Picture the Past
WORK

Jane Shuter

Heinemann
LIBRARY

First published in Great Britain by Heinemann Library
Halley Court, Jordan Hill, Oxford OX2 8EJ
a division of Reed Educational & Professional Publishing Ltd

OXFORD FLORENCE PRAGUE MADRID ATHENS
MELBOURNE AUCKLAND KUALA LUMPUR SINGAPORE TOKYO
IBADAN NAIROBI KAMPALA JOHANNESBURG GABORONE
PORTSMOUTH NH (USA) CHICAGO MEXICO CITY SAO PAULO

Designed by Ken Vail Graphic Design, Cambridge
Colour separations by Dot Gradations, Wickford, Essex
Printed in Malaysia by Times Offset (M) Sdn. Bhd.

01 00 99 98 97
10 9 8 7 6 5 4 3 2 1

ISBN 0 431 04260 8

British Library Cataloguing in Publication Data

Shuter, Jane
  Work – (Picture the past)
  1. Work – History – Juvenile literature
  2. Work – Pictorial works – Juvenile literature
  I. Title
  331

Acknowledgements
The authors and publishers would like to thank the following for permission to use
photographs and other illustrative material:
Beck Isle Museum, page 4 top;
Oxfordshire Photographic Archive, page 18;
Shropshire County Record Office, page 10;
Suffolk Photographic Survey, page 14;
The Imperial War Museum, page 16;
The Mansell Collection, page 12;
The Peter Gillies Collection, page 4 bottom;
The Rural History Centre, Reading University, page 5;
Topham Picturepoint, pages 6, 8, 20.

Cover photographs reproduced with permission of Shropshire County Record Office,
Imperial War Museum and Topham Picturepoint.

Our thanks to Betty Root for her comments in the preparation of this book.

Every effort has been made to contact copyright holders of any material reproduced
in this book. Any omissions will be rectified in subsequent printings if notice is
given to the Publisher.

Contents

Some words are shown in bold text, **like this**. You can find out what these words mean by looking in the glossary on page 24.

Taking photos

People started taking photos in the 1830s. It took over an hour to take a photo! By the 1860s it only took 15 minutes.

When cameras were first invented, they could only take black and white photos. If people wanted colour photos, they had to paint them by hand.

This picture shows **blacksmiths** working in about 1880. The photo was probably taken to show all the different stages of making things with iron.

Builders at work in 1866

The builders in this photo are digging out one of the first London Underground railway lines, the Circle Line.

The builders are using hand **carts** to move heavy loads.

They are using a **pulley** to lower boxes full of bricks and tools to the bottom.

A horse and cart brings bricks and heavy loads to the building site.

Can you find
- how the men got down the hole?
- buckets of water ready to lower?
- bricks to make the tunnel walls?

Shearing sheep in 1880

These farm workers are shearing sheep.
They are cutting the wool off. It does
not hurt the sheep. It is just like having
a haircut.

The men cut the wool off with shears, a tool which cuts like scissors.

The wool comes off in one piece, called a fleece.

This man is treading on the fleeces to squash them into a big sack.

Can you find
- the sheep waiting to be sheared?
- something to drink keeping cold in a bucket of water?
- the sheepdog?

Servants in 1890

These servants worked in a doctor's house. Each of them is holding something that tells us what their job was.

The housekeeper is the best dressed. She told the servants what to do.

The gardener is holding a plant. The boy who helped him has a broom.

The boot boy cleaned the boots and shoes and fetched the coal.

Can you find

- the cook?
- the boy who helped the gardener?
- the **coachman** (he has a whip to drive the horses)?

Post office workers in 1900

These people worked at Shifnal post office. Dan Hall, who owned the post office and shop, is standing in the doorway on the left.

Arthur Bailey collected the post from Newport each night in the horse and **cart**.

The postmen carried letters round the village in big bags.

Parcels were delivered by hand cart.

Can you find

- the postmen's dogs?
- what Dan Hall sold in his shop?
- what the parcels were put in when they were on the cart?

Making carts in 1908

These workers are making **carts**. There is a farm cart and there are some carts for **passengers**. They will all be pulled by horses.

The seats were made of metal. They felt very hard.

Each worker built one cart from start to finish.

The cart was balanced on wooden frames until the wheels were put on.

Can you find

- the racks used to store the workers' tools?
- the lamps on one of the carts?
- how many carts are being made?

Working in the war, 1917

In 1914 a war began. Many men went off to fight. Women had to do the work that men had been doing. These women are working in a factory. They are making **shells** and parts of bombs.

The women wore hats to stop their hair getting caught in the machines.

The women are making **brass nose cones** for the shells.

The brass that was cut off was melted down and used again.

Can you find

- the finished nose cones?
- the big strap that turned to work the machines?
- how the factory was lit?

A telegraph office in 1920

These people worked in the Oxford **telegraph office**. They took messages (called telegrams) for people in Oxford. They sent telegrams too.

This machine used electricity to send the messages. The workers tapped out the messages in code.

This machine printed out the messages that came to the office.

Can you find

- the man who ran the office at his big desk?
- a message that has been sent, hanging on a hook on a wire basket?

Making cars in 1946

These men are making cars in a factory.
They work together to make lots of cars
in one day.

The car seats were made of metal. They were padded and given plastic covers.

Each worker did one job on each car. This man is putting the seats in.

This man is checking that the jobs have been done properly.

What's different?

Look at the photo on page 14. What is different in 1946? Think about:

- how many carts/cars are being made
- how the work is being done.

Did you find?

Builders at work in
1866, pages 6–7

Shearing sheep in
1880, pages 8–9

Servants in 1890,
pages 10–11

Post office workers
in 1900,
pages 12–13

Making carts in
1908, pages 14–15
● six carts

Working in the
war, pages 16–17

A telegraph office
in 1920,
pages 18–19

Glossary (What words mean)

blacksmiths people who make things from metal, like horseshoes, nails and chains

brass a soft metal made from mixing copper and zinc

carts we have used this word for all the horse-drawn vehicles in this book. Passenger vehicles had many names, like gig, donkey cart and carriage.

coachman person whose job is to drive other people in horse-drawn vehicles

nose cones end pieces fitted onto shells or bombs

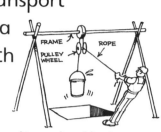

passengers people who are taken from one place to another by some sort of transport

pulley a wheel in a frame, used with a rope to lift heavy loads

shell a large exploding bullet that is shot from a big gun

telegraph office place where telegrams come to and are sent from. Telegrams were sent from one machine to another by someone tapping out a special code.

Index